one happy little songbird

Written and Illustrated by Neil Rabens

ISBN: 0-87239-361-5

 STANDARD PUBLISHING
Cincinnati, Ohio   3631

One little songbird, happy as can be,
Singing of God's love for me.

Two little bunnies, soft and sweet,
God provides for them to eat.

Three little horses having fun,
God made them to prance and run.

Four little beavers cutting wood,
Show that God is kind and good.

Five little squirrels sleep in a tree,
The home God made for them, you see.

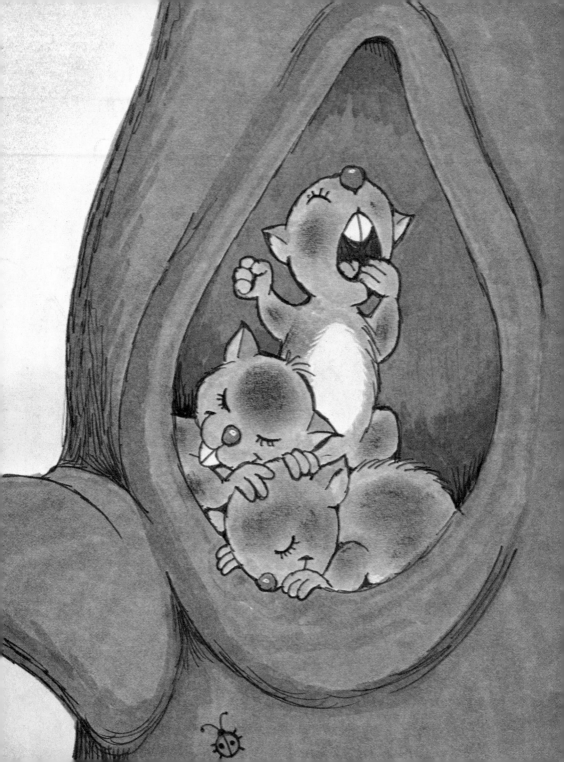

Let's keep counting. It's such fun
To see what all the Lord has done.

Six little ducklings
wait for rain.
God will make it
come again.

Seven little chipmunks look for seeds
God provides for all their needs.

Eight little puppies playing ball,
God made some big and others small.

Nine little frogs so very proud,
God gave them voices clear and loud.

Ten little children kneel and pray,
God hears every word they say.

We have thought of thy loving-kindness, O God. Psalm 48:9